OUR GRE★T STATES

WHAT'S GREAT ABOUT
DELAWARE?

✳ Sheri Dillard

LERNER PUBLICATIONS ✳ MINNEAPOLIS

CONTENTS

DELAWARE WELCOMES YOU! * 4

Copyright © 2016
by Lerner Publishing Group, Inc.

Content Consultant: Lynn W. Moore, History
Chair, Wilmington University

Lerner Publications Company
A division of Lerner Publishing Group, Inc.
241 First Avenue North
Minneapolis, MN 55401 USA

For reading levels and more information, look
up this title at www.lernerbooks.com.

Main body text set in ITC Franklin Gothic Std
Book Condensed 12/15.
Typeface provided by Adobe Systems.

**Library of Congress Cataloging-in-Publication
Data**

The Cataloging-in-Publication Data for *What's
Great about Delaware?* is on file at the Library
of Congress.
ISBN 978-1-4677-3874-3 (lib. bdg.)
ISBN 978-1-4677-8493-1 (pbk.)
ISBN 978-1-4677-8494-8 (EB pdf)

Manufactured in the United States of America
1 – PC – 7/15/15

DELAWARE Welcomes You!

Welcome to Delaware—the first state! Delaware may be small, but it is packed full of fun things to see and do. Delaware has many miles of ocean beaches. Jump in for a swim, skimboard along the shoreline, or kayak with dolphins. For a different kind of thrill, head to Dover International Speedway to hear the roar of racecar engines. Or jump on a bike for a race of your own down one of the state's many trails. From quiet strolls through a wildlife refuge to wild rides on the boardwalk, Delaware has something for everyone. Read on to discover ten things that make Delaware great. Whether it's your first visit or your fiftieth, you are sure to have fun in our nation's first state!

PENNSYLVANIA

Hockessin
Wilmington
Pike Creek
Ebright Azimuth
(448 feet / 137 m)
Newark
Brookside
Bear
Glasgow
Pea Patch
Island

NEW
JERSEY

Middletown

Delaware River

Smyrna

Dover

Delaware
Bay

MARYLAND

Rehoboth
Bay

Nanticoke River

ATLANTIC OCEAN

Miles
0   5   10   15
0   10   20
Kilometers

Explore Delaware's beaches and all the places in between! Just turn the page to find out all about the FIRST STATE. >

REHOBOTH BEACH

Try out one of the many video games at Funland on the boardwalk.

> If you're visiting Delaware in the summer months, head to the beach! The city of Rehoboth Beach is a popular spot. Here you can swim, snorkel, or surf in the Atlantic Ocean. Try skimboarding if you're looking for a new activity. Take a running jump onto your skimboard as you zip into the ocean. The crashing waves bring you back on the beach. You can learn some cool tricks at the East Coast Skimboarding Championships. They are held at nearby Dewey Beach each summer.

Make sure to visit the boardwalk. It is steps from the beach. Grab a slice of pizza or try some saltwater taffy. Stop at Funland, the boardwalk's amusement park. The park has nineteen rides to choose from, including bumper cars and a carousel. Be sure to check out the arcade for Skee-Ball, video games, and pinball machines. Maybe you'll be lucky and win prizes!

After a day at the beach, explore Jungle Jim's. It is Delaware's largest water park. Race down a waterslide or relax and float along the lazy river. The park also has bumper boats and go-karts to ride.

How big a sandcastle can you build at the beach?

CAPE HENLOPEN STATE PARK

> Cape Henlopen State Park in Lewes is a popular stop for outdoor fun. Sign up for a 1- to 3-mile (2- to 5-kilometer) guided kayak tour. Or you can rent kayaks and explore on your own. Delaware Bay is a perfect spot to see dolphins and whales. Even if you don't spot these animals, you'll likely see a school of fish or some horseshoe crabs.

If you prefer to stay on land, try hiking or biking the park's paved trails. Stop at Fort Miles, used to defend the region during World War II (1939–1945). Take a quick tour and look out for German boats from one of the towers, just as the soldiers did.

Continue on the trails to the Seaside Nature Center. Look inside five different 1,000-gallon (3,785-liter) fish tanks. How many types of local fish can you find? You can also stop at the touch tank to see and touch marine life. Don't forget to check out the Osprey Cam! In the spring, watch video from this live feed to see chicks hatch from their eggs and grow. Map out where the hawks will fly during the winter and the summer.

LEWES, DELAWARE

The town of Lewes was founded in 1631. It was the first settlement founded in Delaware, which was the first state in the United States. Delaware was one of the thirteen original states to approve the US Constitution. It became a state on December 7, 1787.

Horseshoe crabs use their tails to move through the sand near Delaware Bay.

DOVER INTERNATIONAL SPEEDWAY

> Start your engines and race to Dover International Speedway! This 1-mile (2 km) racetrack is known as the Monster Mile. The track hosts two NASCAR events each year. The drivers zoom around the track and reach speeds of more than 150 miles (240 km) per hour.

Arrive early on race day and have your picture taken outside the speedway with Miles the Monster. Then make your way to the FanZone. Listen to live music and check out the race cars on display. You can even pretend to drive a race car in a simulator. Sometimes you can meet drivers in the FanZone. Wait in line for their autographs. Then visit the Monster FunZone. Choose from rides, a bounce house, and a rock-climbing wall.

Miles the Monster stands 46 feet (14 meters) tall outside Dover International Speedway!

If you're lucky, you can get your favorite driver's autograph at the FanZone!

WORLD CHAMPIONSHIP PUNKIN CHUNKIN CONTEST

> Get ready for fall fun when you visit the World Championship Punkin Chunkin contest in Dover. This contest is held around Halloween. In the past, more than twenty thousand visitors have attended to see who can launch a pumpkin the farthest. The participants use homemade catapults and air cannons. One year, a pumpkin traveled almost 4,700 feet (1,433 m)! Want to give it a try? Sign up for the youth contest. Pick your pumpkin carefully!

After you've seen enough pumpkin hurling, listen and dance to live music. Or try chili from the chili cook-off. Pick your favorite. You can also choose from more than twenty other kinds of foods. Maybe you'd like pumpkin-flavored foods or turkey legs. Walk through the grounds to see the arts and crafts for sale. Play games or take a ride on a mechanical bull. Then settle in for the fireworks show!

Pick out your favorite pumpkin at the World Championship Punkin Chunkin contest.

DELAWARE'S CROPS AND ANIMALS

Delaware farmers grow many different fruits and vegetables. Pumpkins are just one of the state's crops. Almost 40 percent of Delaware's land is used for farming. Other major crops grown in the state include corn, soybeans, and apples. Delaware is also one of the top-producing poultry states in the country. Many crops stay in the state, but others are shipped across the country.

Stop at the Amish schoolhouse to try pie or cookies baked by local Amish families.

AMISH COUNTRY BIKE TOUR

> Delaware is a great state for biking. And the long-running Amish Country Bike Tour in Dover is a fun way to see why! More than two thousand cyclists from twenty-five states participate each year. You can join in the fun! How far do you want to ride? Choose from a 15-mile (24 km) ride up to a 100-mile (160 km) course.

When you're set to begin your ride, park your bike behind the Amish horse and buggy at the starting line. Then wait for the starting gun. Enjoy your ride through Dover, farmland, and small Amish communities. Wave to the fans cheering you on!

If you're getting hungry on your ride, pause at one of many rest stops. Choose from healthful snacks, sandwiches, and water. A favorite stop among riders is the Amish schoolhouse for a sweet treat. Yum! At the end of the race, join in the barbecue feast.

AMISH COMMUNITY

There is a large Amish community in Delaware. The Amish are a peaceful religious group. Many Amish families moved to the East Coast from Switzerland in the 1700s. From the founding of the religion until modern times, Amish people have been known for leading simple lives. They do not use cars or electricity. In parts of Delaware, it is common to see an Amish family riding in a horse-drawn buggy.

FORT DELAWARE STATE PARK

> Make your way to Delaware City next. Here you'll hop aboard a ferry for a short ride to Pea Patch Island. A small bus will then take you to Fort Delaware. Union soldiers used this fortress during the Civil War (1861–1865). The fort held prisoners of war.

Follow your tour guide as you explore the fortress. All the workers wear historical clothing. You'll feel as if you have stepped back in time! During your visit, stop at the blacksmith's shop. If you're lucky, you can try using his hammer to help build a cannon. Or maybe you'll get to help clean the town's laundry. Try out an old-fashioned washboard. Then watch the soldiers practice firing guns and muskets. Listen to prisoners tell their stories of trying to escape. Some were successful, while others were not.

If you're visiting in September, pitch a tent and stay overnight. Bring your flashlight for a nighttime scavenger hunt. Then head over to the campfire for s'mores and ghost stories. Maybe you can go on your own ghost hunt!

Visit Fort Delaware's blacksmith (*above*) and laundress (*below*) and help them with their work.

BOMBAY HOOK
NATIONAL WILDLIFE REFUGE

> Bombay Hook National Wildlife Refuge near Smyrna is the largest refuge in the state. It is a great place to see migrating birds and other wildlife. More than 150,000 ducks and geese fly through this area each fall.

Start your day at the visitor center. Here you'll find information about birds, trail maps, and wildlife checklists that you can use throughout your visit. Then hop in the car for a 12-mile (19 km) wildlife drive. You'll stop at walking trails, pools, and observation towers along the way.

The Boardwalk Trail will lead you to the first tower. Once you reach the top of this 30-foot (9 m) tower, look down on Raymond Pool. How many different birds do you see? Be sure to mark them off your checklist! Or stop at one of the Bird Identification Stations along the drive. Peer through the binoculars. You may see small songbirds or giant bald eagles!

Join an education class at Bombay Hook to learn about marsh plants and animals.

TIDAL SALT MARSHES

Most of Bombay Hook is a tidal salt marsh. Tidal salt marshes are wetlands along ocean coasts. The tides repeatedly flood the area with saltwater, which then drains away. Bombay Hook's staff works hard to keep pollution out of the salt marshes. Many staff members do research in the refuge. They can learn more about Delaware's birds and other wildlife here.

WINTERTHUR

> Be sure to visit Winterthur near Wilmington. This estate, built in the 1830s, was the former home of the du Pont family. The family fled France and started several companies in the United States. These days, it is a museum with outdoor gardens, meadows, and forests to explore. Sign up for one of many tour options. The introductory guided tour will lead you through some of the 175 rooms in the house. You'll see a dining room, the drawing room, and a few bedrooms.

After your tour, make your way back to the first floor. Stop in the Touch-It Room and choose one of the hands-on activities. Try on clothes similar to what children wore in the 1700s. Then have a tea party in the parlor room. Or you can play with toys and puzzles from early American life. Then go shopping in the 1830s general store. You can pretend to cook a feast in the kitchen.

Make your way outside to explore the Enchanted Woods. Take a tram ride with stops along the way. You may find the perfect spot for a picnic lunch. Listen for frogs, birds, and chipmunks while you eat.

Explore the Faerie Cottage in Winterthur's Enchanted Woods.

You can't miss the bright yellow building of the Delaware Children's Museum!

DELAWARE CHILDREN'S MUSEUM

> Head toward the riverfront in Wilmington and look for the giant yellow Delaware Children's Museum. Once inside, create your own building in the Structures room. Trace a design created by an architect. Or build your own creation with large blocks and other materials. Will your building hold up in an earthquake? Test it and see!

Next, discover the power of your body in the Power of Me exhibit. See how long you can hold yourself up on the chin-up bar. Then climb to the top of the rock wall as fast as you can. Try out the rowing machine too.

Spend time at the hands-on stream table. Here you can explore how water travels through locks. You'll also learn about wind power. Stop in the Bank on It room to learn more about money. Try using the ATM and writing a check! And don't miss the Touch Tank Aquarium. You can get close to marine life such as rays and fish.

If you're looking for a challenge, check out the 30-foot (9-m) climbing structure in the museum lobby.

DELAWARE STATE FAIR

Enjoy some fair food (*top*) or a concert (*bottom*) at the Delaware State Fair.

> For ten days each summer, the Delaware State Fair in Harrington comes to life with music, food, and carnival rides. More than three hundred thousand people have attended in past years! The fair began in 1919 and has grown each year. It has something for everyone!

Walk around the fairgrounds to find your favorite foods. Maybe you'll munch on a corn dog, cotton candy, or ice cream. While you're enjoying your snack, check out the day's events. You might see pig races, a rodeo, or a demolition derby. Get your spot for the daily parade and listen to local marching bands play. Or maybe you'll go to a concert! There are live concerts every day with big names such as Keith Urban and Taylor Swift.

One of the most popular attractions is the carnival. Choose from more than thirty rides, including bumper boats, roller coasters, and a Ferris wheel. You'll find plenty to keep you busy! After a long day of fun, be sure to save some energy for the fireworks show!

You have read about ten awesome things to see and do in Delaware. Now, think about what your Delaware top ten list would include. What would you like to see if you visited the state? What would you like to do there? What activities are most exciting to you? What would you tell your friends to do if they visited Delaware? Keep these things in mind as you make your own top ten list.

DELAWARE BY MAP

> ## MAP KEY

 Capital city

◯ City

◯ Point of interest

▲ Highest elevation

–·– State border

Visit www.lerneresource.com to learn more about the state flag of Delaware.

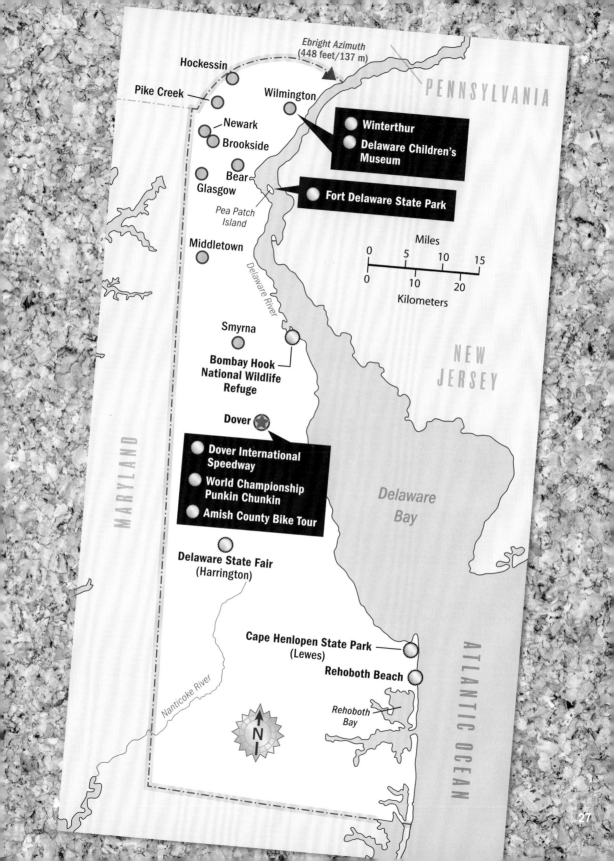

Ebright Azimuth
(448 feet/137 m)

PENNSYLVANIA

Hockessin

Pike Creek

Wilmington

Winterthur

Delaware Children's Museum

Newark

Brookside

Bear

Glasgow

Fort Delaware State Park

Pea Patch Island

Middletown

Delaware River

Miles
0   5   10   15
0   10   20
Kilometers

Smyrna

Bombay Hook National Wildlife Refuge

NEW JERSEY

Dover

Dover International Speedway

World Championship Punkin Chunkin

Amish County Bike Tour

Delaware Bay

MARYLAND

Delaware State Fair (Harrington)

Cape Henlopen State Park (Lewes)

Rehoboth Beach

ATLANTIC OCEAN

Nanticoke River

Rehoboth Bay

N

27

DELAWARE FACTS

NICKNAME: The First State

SONG: "Our Delaware" by George B. Hynson and William M. S. Brown

MOTTO: "Liberty and Independence"

FLOWER: peach blossom

TREE: American holly

BIRD: blue hen chicken

ANIMALS: gray fox, horseshoe crab

FOOD: peach pie

DATE AND RANK OF STATEHOOD: December 7, 1787; the 1st state

CAPITAL: Dover

AREA: 2,023 square miles (5,240 sq. km)

AVERAGE JANUARY TEMPERATURE: 35°F (2°C)

AVERAGE JULY TEMPERATURE: 76°F (24°C)

POPULATION AND RANK: 925,749; 45th (2013)

MAJOR CITIES AND POPULATIONS: Wilmington (71,525), Dover (37,366), Newark (32,549), Middletown (19,600), Bear (19,371)

NUMBER OF US CONGRESS MEMBERS: 1 representative, 2 senators

NUMBER OF ELECTORAL VOTES: 3

NATURAL RESOURCES: magnesium, sand, gravel

AGRICULTURAL PRODUCTS: corn, milk, poultry, soybeans, wheat

MANUFACTURED GOODS: chemicals, computer and electronic products, food products

STATE HOLIDAYS OR CELEBRATIONS: Delaware State Fair, World Championship Punkin Chunkin, Return Day

GLOSSARY

architect: someone who designs buildings

blacksmith: someone who makes things from iron by heating it and hammering it into shape

catapult: a device used for launching items through the air

fortress: a place that is strong to protect against attack

refuge: an area that provides protection or shelter

simulator: a machine used to show what something looks and feels like

skimboard: a small surfboard-like board for riding in shallow water along the beach

wetland: land with a lot of moisture, such as a marsh or a swamp

FURTHER INFORMATION

Delaware Facts and Symbols
http://www.delaware.gov/topics/facts/index.shtml
Explore the importance of Delaware's state symbols at this website.

Delaware State Parks
http://www.destateparks.com
This site has all the information you'll need when you visit one of Delaware's many state parks.

Downey, Tika. *Delaware: The First State*. New York: PowerKids, 2010. Learn more about Delaware's geography, weather, and businesses in this book.

For Kids: Delaware
http://www.ipl.org/div/stateknow/de1.html
Visit this site for fun facts about the state of Delaware, as well as some of its famous people.

Ransom, Candice. *Who Wrote the US Constitution? And Other Questions about the Constitutional Convention of 1787*. Minneapolis: Lerner Publications, 2011. Delaware was the first state in the nation to ratify the US Constitution. This book will answer key questions about that document's history.

Wolny, Philip. *Delaware: Past and Present*. New York: Rosen Central, 2010. This book covers the interesting history and people of Delaware.

INDEX

PHOTO ACKNOWLEDGMENTS

The images in this book are used with the permission of: © Songquan Deng/Shutterstock Images, p. 1; NASA, pp. 2–3; © American Spirit/Shutterstock Images, p. 4; © Laura Westlund/Independent Picture Service, pp. 5, 27; © Yvonne Navalaney/Shutterstock Images, p. 5; © Ian Dagnall/Alamy, pp. 6–7; © National Geographic Image Collection/Alamy, p. 6; © oliveromg/Shutterstock Images, p. 7; © aimintang/iStockphoto, pp. 8–9; © North Wind Picture Archives/Alamy, p. 9 (top); © Jana Shea/Shutterstock Images, p. 9 (bottom); © Action Sports Photography/Shutterstock Images, pp. 10–11; © Matthew O'Haren/Icon Sportswire, p. 11 (top); © Walter G. Arce/ASP/Cal Sport Media/Newscom, p. 11 (bottom); © Chris Connelly CC 2.0, pp. 12–13; © Blend Images/Shutterstock Images, p. 13 (top); © monticello/Shutterstock Images, p. 13 (bottom); © C.M. Baker/Kent County Tourism, pp. 14–15, 14; © Christian Kieffer/Shutterstock Images, p. 15; © combatphoto44 CC 2.0, pp. 16–17; © Mathieu Plourde CC 2.0, p. 17 (top); © Herb Quick/Alamy, p. 17 (bottom); © US Fish and Wildlife Service CC 2.0, pp. 18–19, 19 (left); © Jay CC 2.0, p. 19 (right); © Jim, the Photographer CC 2.0, pp. 20–21, 21; © Ethan Daniels/Shutterstock Images, pp. 22–23; © Emory Hill CC 2.0, p. 23; © i-m-a-g-e/Shutterstock Images, pp. 24–25; © Owen Sweeney/Invision/AP Images, p. 24 (bottom); © TFoxFoto/Shutterstock Images, p. 24 (top); © nicoolay/iStockphoto, p. 26; © Vasilius/Shutterstock Images, p. 29 (top); © visceralimage/Shutterstock Images, p. 29 (middle left); © sframephoto/iStockphoto, p. 29 (middle right); © smereka/Shutterstock Images, p. 29 (bottom).

Front cover: © Greg Dale/Getty Images (beach); © RoJo Images/Shutterstock.com (peach pie); © goccedicolore.it/Shutterstock.com (peach blossoms); © age fotostock/SuperStock (fair); © Laura Westlund/Independent Picture Service (map); © iStockphoto.com/fpm (seal); © iStockphoto.com/vicm (pushpins); © iStockphoto.com/benz190 (corkboard).